The Formation of the
Albanian National Consciousness

A.K. Brackob

The Formation of the
Albanian National Consciousness

VITA HISTRIA

Vita Histria

Las Vegas ◊ Oxford ◊ Palm Beach

Published in the United States of America by
Histria Books, a division of Histria LLC
7181 N. Hualapai Way, Suite 130-86
Las Vegas, NV 89166 USA
HistriaBooks.com

Vita Histria is an imprint of Histria Books. Titles
published under the imprints of Histria Books are
distributed worldwide.

Library of Congress Control Number 2020952127

ISBN 978-1-59211-050-6 (hardcover)
ISBN 978-1-59211-146-6 (soft bound)

Table of Contents

In Memory of

Dr. Keith Hitchins

Scholar, Mentor, and Friend

The Formation of the
Albanian National Consciousness

Introduction

I n the fall of 1879, the English barrister Edward Knight was deciding how to spend his upcoming vacation when a friend offered him the opportunity to join a small expedition to what the renowned historian Edward Gibbon once referred to as the remotest part of Europe – Albania. He quickly accepted the chance to participate in this exotic adventure. "I myself knew nothing about Albania before starting," Knight wrote, "with the exception of what I had gleaned from 'Childe Harold.' The lines where the poet sings,

> *Albania, rugged nurse of savage men,*

came to mind, so I took down Byron from my shelves, and read all that he has to say about

> *The wild Albanian kirtled to his knee,*
> *With shawl-girt head, and ornamented gun*
> *And gold-embroider'd garments fair to see.*

The information was scanty, but sufficient to show me that no more interesting country could have been chosen for our expedition."[1]

Knight was not to be disappointed. At the time of his journey, the Albanians were engaged in a struggle to oppose the implementation of the decisions of the Congress of Berlin which awarded portions of Albanian territory to Serbia, Montenegro, and Greece. To achieve this end, on 10 June 1878, the Albanians created the League of Prizren. Through this organized resistance, they served notice on the Great Powers of Europe that the Albanian nationality could not be ignored in any resolution to the so-called 'Eastern Question.'[2]

The determined resistance of the Albanians to the partitioning of their lands following the Russo-Turkish War of 1877-1878 made it clear that a national awakening was underway. Edward Knight's experience in Albania confirmed this: "The world will hear a good deal of the doings of this Albanian League someday...," he wrote. "The chiefs of the association are, I believe, honest men, patriotic, and determined to carry out their programme

---

[1]Edward Knight, *Albania: A Narrative of Recent Travel* (London, 1880), p. 2.

[2]Arben Puto, "La ligue albanaise et la crise orientale," pp. 95-116 in *Studia Albanica*, 15:1 (1978), p. 115.

Prizren, the meeting place of the Albanian League in 1878

to the death."[3] The armed resistance of the League forced the Congress of Berlin to twice alter its territorial settlement between the Ottoman Empire and Montenegro. In so doing, it forced the Great Powers to recognize the Albanian question for the first time. Though there were many trials and tribulations to be faced before Albania would gain independence in 1912, the creation of the League of Prizren marked a decisive moment in Albanian history.

Knight was one of the few Europeans of that time who realized that the League of Prizren was a

---

[3]Knight, p. 258.

manifestation of the Albanian national consciousness. German Chancellor Otto von Bismarck shunned Albanian protests to the Congress of Berlin declaring, "There is no Albanian nationality!"[4] For a variety of political purposes, the very fact that an Albanian national awakening ever occurred has occasionally been denied. For example, Panagiotes Pipineles, in a polemic aimed at pressing Greek claims to the territory of southern Albania in 1963, quoted a French journalist who in the early 1900s wrote:

> it is not true that there is an Albanian people which aspires to autonomy or independence. I would go further and declare that there is no such thing as an Albanian people. Of course, there is an Albanian race, but everything which goes to make up a nationality is wanting.[5]

Fortunately, most scholars have not been this naïve. Many, however, have argued that it was only in response to the threatened partitioning of their lands by the Treaty of San Stefano and the Congress of Berlin that the

---

[4]quoted in Constantine A. Chekrezi, *Albania: Past and Present,* (New York, 1919), p. 51.

[5]Quoted in Panagiotes Pipeneles, *Europe and the Albanian Question* (Chicago, 1963), p. 22.

The Shkodra delegation to the League of Prizren

Albanians began to develop a national consciousness.[6] This interpretation is wrong. The formation of the Albanian national consciousness did not suddenly occur in 1878. As in the case of other Balkan peoples, it gradually developed throughout the nineteenth century.

Albanian historians refer to this period as the National Renaissance. Had a national consciousness not taken shape prior to the crisis of 1878, the creation of a national movement which not only sought to protect Albanian lands against foreign annexation, but also strove to unite the four Albanian vilayets into a single

---

[6]Frederic Gilbert, *Les pays d'Albanie et leur histoire* (Paris, 1914), p. 275; Stanford Shaw, *History of the Ottoman Empire and Modern Turkey*, volume 2 (New York, 1976), p. 199; and Chekrezi, p. 51.

autonomous administrative unit, would not have been possible. The development of a national consciousness during the decades preceding 1878 created the foundation upon which this national movement was built. Beginning with this premise, my purpose is to examine the formation of the Albanian national consciousness which culminated in the creation of the League of Prizren and ultimately led to the formation of an independent Albanian nation-state in 1912.

Although research for this project was begun many years ago, the publication of this book was inspired by a question posed on a popular internet site, where it was asked, "Would Albania exist if not for the Ottomans?" To me, this question revealed a profound lack of knowledge about Albanian history and culture. My answer, simply put, was that Albania exists despite the Ottomans. As this book will demonstrate, the Albanian people have a unique history and culture. They have bravely preserved their national identity despite all foreign attempts to subjugate and assimilate them, including, most famously, by the Ottoman Empire.

This small book is intended as an introductory companion to Stavro Skendi's masterful work, *The Albanian National Awakening*, which is a comprehensive study of the period from the creation of the League of Prizren to the founding of the Albanian national state amidst the Balkan Wars and the collapse of the Ottoman Empire.

I am grateful to Dr. Keith Hitchins of the University of Illinois at Urbana-Champaign for his inspiration and guidance during the time that the research for this project was initially conducted. His recent passing was a profound loss to all those who knew him, and I dedicate this book in his memory.

I

Ethnic Identity
and National Consciousness

The awareness of an ethnic identity is a necessary prerequisite to the development of a national consciousness. A group becomes aware of its ethnic identity when it recognizes that its language, customs, and traditions are distinct from those of neighboring peoples. This does not imply that it was the principal mode by which people identified themselves. Indeed, it was not. In pre-modern rural societies, familial ties, the village community, the local region, and in some cases religion were far more important to peasants as means of self-identification.

Once a group acquires a sense of ethnic identity, it holds the potential of developing a national consciousness. There is no necessity to this transformation; a wide range of regional and local variables, including geography, history, culture, and social and economic development, help determine when, or if, it will occur. A national consciousness is forged when people start to look beyond the local and regional differences separating them and begin to identify themselves and their place in the world primarily in terms of their ethnic identity.

The Albanians are the descendants of the ancient Illyrians who inhabited the Balkan peninsula since pre-Homeric times. The antiquity of the people in their homeland is an important element in the Albanian ethnic identity as they are distinguished by being the oldest inhabitants of the peninsula and because they speak a language, derived from ancient Illyrian, distinct from that of their Slavic and Greek neighbors. Only in the fifteenth century, however, did a sense of ethnic identity develop among the Albanians during their resistance to the Ottoman invasions. This resistance, led by George Castriota Scanderbeg, brought Albanians of various regions, speaking different dialects, together in a common struggle against foreign aggression. This struggle helped define the ethnic identity of the Albanians. In book VI of his *Commentaries*, Pope Pius II cites a letter ostensibly written by Scanderbeg and sent to the Prince of Taranto that helps to illustrate this sense of ethnic awareness:

> Our ancestors were Epirotes, of whom came that Pyrrhus whose attack the Romans could hardly resist, who took by force of arms Tarentum and many other Italian towns. You cannot set against

the valiant Epirotes the Tarentines, a sodden race born to catch fish. If you say that Albania is part of Macedonia, you concede us far nobler ancestors, who penetrated with Alexander into India, laying low with incredible success all the nations who opposed them.[7]

Whether or not the letter itself is authentic, the sentiment it expressed certainly is. Albanians recognized that they were a distinct group of people with a unique heritage.

Scanderbeg himself became the focus of this ethnic identity. His twenty-five-year resistance to the Ottoman invasions forged a sense of unity among the Albanians. Even for peasants in those areas of the country that did not participate in Scanderbeg's revolt, he symbolized their struggle against foreign and domestic oppressions and they kept his memory alive. This was readily apparent during the Albanian rebellion of 1481. The region of Himara, south of Vlora on the Adriatic coast, where the rebellion began, had never been under Scanderbeg's control; yet, when the rebellion broke out, they sent representatives to the Kingdom of Naples to recall Scanderbeg's son, John Castriota, from Italy to lead the revolt. Upon his return to Albania, all of the liberated

---

[7]Pius II, "The Commentaries of Pius II: Book VI-IX," trans. Florence Alden Gragg, *Smith College Studies in History*, Volume 35 (North Hampton, MA, 1951), p. 460.

George Castriota Scanderbeg

areas of the country recognized John Castriota as their prince.[8]

The Ottoman conquest of Albania during the fifteenth century ushered in four and a half centuries of foreign domination. Ottoman rule could not, however, destroy the sense of ethnic awareness that had developed in the fifteenth century. Albanians steadfastly preserved their language, culture, and traditions. Edward Knight was struck by the fact that, "The Turks have never assimilated the remoter possessions... They seem, even after so many centuries, to be merely temporarily encamped in Albania."[9]

The geographic isolation provided by the mountains helped preserve their traditional way of life throughout the centuries of Ottoman domination. As the British scholar Margaret Hasluck rightly pointed out, the Turks, "could never exert more than a nominal authority outside the chief towns. If they sent a punitive column into the interior, the people living in the mountains took evasive action, retreating to some peak until the

---

[8]Stefano Magno, "Événements historique en Grèce (1479-1497)," pp. 214-243 in *Documents inédit relatifs à l'histoire de la Grèce au Moyen Age*, Tome VI, ed. C.N. Sathas (Paris, 1884), p. 229.

[9]Knight, p. 116.

inevitable departure of the intruders; their wealth was so small that they carry or drive off most of it to their refuge, and so lost little from the raid."[10] Despite its long duration and the numerous conversions to Islam, Ottoman rule did not blur the Albanian ethnic identity.

This strong sense of ethnic awareness impressed many foreign visitors to Albania in the early nineteenth century. The scholar William Leake wrote, "it is not probable that the Porte has ever been able to enforce a more implicit obedience to its orders than it now does, when it is unable to appoint or confirm any provincial governor who is not native of Albania, and who has not already established his influence by his arms, policy, and connections."[11] The French consul at Janina, F. Pouqueville, observed that, "they obstinately preserve the Sclavonian [Albanian] language; and though they are in great degree expatriated, they are proud of the name of Albanians, their national appellation."[12] Likewise, John Cam Hobhouse, who accompanied Lord Byron on

---

[10]Margaret Hasluck, *The Unwritten Law in Albania,* ed. J.H. Hutton (Cambridge, 1954), p.9.

[11]William Martin Leake, *Researches in Greece* (London, 1814), p. 250.

[12]F.C.H.L. Pouqueville, *Travels through the Morea, Albania and several other parts of the Ottoman Empire to Constantinople during the years 1798, 1799, 1800 and 1801* (London, 1806), p. 189.

his journey to the Ottoman lands, remarked of the Albanians:

> There is a spirit of independence and a love of their country, in the whole people, that, in a great measure, does away with the vast distinction, observable in other parts of Turkey, between the followers of the two religions. For when natives of other provinces, upon being asked who they are, will say, 'we are Turks' or, 'we are Christians,' a man of this country answers, 'I am an Albanian.'[13]

This strong sense of ethnic identity evident in the early nineteenth century formed the basis for the development of the Albanian national consciousness.

---

[13]John Cam Hobhouse, *A Journey through Albania and other Provinces of Turkey in Europe and Asia, to Constantinople, during the years 1809 and 1810* (London, 1813), pp. 147-148.

II

Threats to the Albanian Ethnic Identity

W hat factors cause the development of a national consciousness? There can be no simple answer to this question; in any particular instance, a number of different factors can be identified. Among the Albanians, the driving force in the development of national consciousness was the strong desire to preserve their ethnic individuality against the external forces that threatened to destroy their language and customs. The Albanian nationalist Pashko Vasa clearly indicated this when he wrote:

> We do not want the Albanian people to lose their characteristic type, their customs, their legends and their language. These are the only riches that

our fathers bequeathed us. We wish to conserve them."[14]

Among the forces that threatened to destroy the Albanian language and culture was the rise of national consciousness among other Balkan peoples. Both the Greeks and Serbians established national states in the early nineteenth century, followed later in the century by the Serbs of Montenegro and the Bulgarians. The Albanians viewed these new states as threats because each made claims to territories traditionally inhabited by Albanians. In addition, as national states, they pursued policies of cultural hegemony and would attempt to assimilate the Albanians into Greek or Slavic culture. Ismail Kemal, the Albanian nationalist who proclaimed the independence of his country in 1912, expressed the feeling of his people when he wrote:

irrespective of their region or religion, they manifested more clearly their conviction of racial individuality, as distinct from that of other people of the Balkans, and affirmed more and more their

---

[14]Wassa Effendi [Pashko Vasa], *Études sur l'Albanie et les Albanais* (Constantinople, 1879), p. 113. Hereafter cited as Vasa, *Études sur l'Albanie.*

decision not to be subjugated by any foreign government, Greek or Slav.[15]

The other threat to Albanian ethnic individuality came from the Tanzimat reforms in the Ottoman Empire that began with the decree of Gülhane in 1839 and continued throughout the century. These reforms sought to increase the centralization of the Empire's administration and expand the role of the state in Ottoman society.[16] The Tanzimat reforms also encouraged the spread of education throughout the Empire. They guaranteed the right of all nationalities to use their own language in their schools and churches, but this right was denied to the Albanians. According to the millet system, they were viewed as Turks or Greeks depending upon their religion or language.[17] The increasing centralization of the Ottoman government impinged upon the traditional autonomy enjoyed in most parts of Albania, while the spread of education in

[15]Ismail Kemal, *The Memoirs of Ismail Kemal Bey*, ed. Sommerville Story, (London, 1920), p. 364.

[16]Shaw, v. 2, p. 55.

[17]Stefanaq Pollo and Arben Puto, *The History of Albania*, trans. Carol Wiseman and Ginnie Hole (London, 1981), pp. 110-114, hereafter cited as Pollo and Puto; Anton Logoreci, *The Albanians; Europe's Forgotten Survivors* (London, 1977), p. 43; and Shaw, v. 2, p. 200.

foreign languages threatened to destroy the traditional culture. The Albanian national consciousness formed in response to these threats.

III

History and National Awakening

A midst this turmoil, the Albanian national renaissance began. History was one of the prominent concerns of the Albanian intellectuals who fostered the awakening of a national consciousness among their people. These intellectuals chiefly concerned themselves with two historical problems – the origins of the Albanian people and the resistance to Ottoman expansion in southeastern Europe led by George Castriota Scanderbeg in the fifteenth century.

As was true of other Balkan peoples, such as the Romanians, the question of the origins of the Albanian people had serious political implications. Naum Veqilharxhi, Jeromin De Rada, Pashko Vasa and other prominent intellectuals advocated the theory that the Albanians were descendants of the Pelasgi, the oldest inhabitants of the Balkan peninsula.[18] The other popular theory, and the one generally accepted today,[19] is that the Albanians were the direct descendants of the ancient Illyrians. Henry Holland, an English traveler to Albania in the early nineteenth century, encountered this view and remarked:

> if the opinion be well founded that the Albanians are descended from the ancient Illyrians, they may be considered as actually inhabiting the country which belonged to their remote ancestors.[20]

Both theories regard the Albanians as indigenous inhabitants of the Balkan peninsula. This point was critical to Albanian nationalists. It proved the autochthony of the people in their lands and thus served as an important political weapon in refuting the claims of neighboring people to portions of Albanian territory.

The question of Albanian origins became especially significant during the crisis of 1878-1881. This problem is

---

[18]Stefanaq Pollo, ed., *Historia e Shqipërisë*, vëlle. 2 (Tiranë, 1984), pp. 139-140. Hereafter cited as *Historia e Shqipërisë*, II.

[19]Pollo and Pollo, pp. 3-4.

[20]Henry Holland, *Travels in the Ionian Isles, Albania, Thessaly, Macedonia, & a. during the years 1812 and 1813*, volume 2 (London, 1819), p. 334.

a central focus of the work of Pashko Vasa (1825-1892), one of the leading Albanian intellectuals of the nineteenth century. Vasa served as secretary to the British consul in Shkodra before moving to Italy where he took part in the Venetian uprising against Austrian rule in 1848. After the Venetian uprising was put down, Vasa fled to the Ottoman Empire where he held various posts in the government and became a leading figure among Albanian nationalists in Istanbul. His book, *Études sur l'Albanie et les Albanais*, is the most important historical work of the Albanian national renaissance; it was published in French and German in 1878 and asserted the national rights of the Albanians and the goals of the League of Prizren to a European audience.[21] One of his principal concerns was to refute Greek claims to the territory of southern Albania, and "to prove the antiquity of the Albanian people and their own existence outside of the Hellenic family."[22] To do this, Vasa argued that the Albanians were the descendants of the ancient Pelasgi, that they inhabited the Balkan peninsula longer than any other people, and that they are an ethnic group distinct from the Greeks.

---

[21]Vasa, *Études sur l'Albanie;* and Vehbi Bala, "Pashko Vasa (1825-1892)" in *Fjalor Enciklopedik Shqiptar* (Tiranë, 1985), p. 1155.

[22]Vasa, *Études sur l'Albanie*, p. 37.

The leading figure of the League of Prizren, Abdyl Frashëri, made a similar appeal to European public opinion when he wrote in *Le Messager de Vienne* on 17 May 1878: "We are not a branch of the Greek nation, but an older nation than the Greeks. Our language has with the Greek language those ties with Sanskrit has with German."[23] These nationalists strove to preserve the territorial integrity of their lands by making Europe aware that the Albanians were a nation distinct from their Balkan neighbors. Thus, the question of the origins of the Albanian people had strong political implications.

George Castriota Scanderbeg and his famous struggle against the Ottoman invaders in the fifteenth century was the other historical topic to which nineteenth century nationalists devoted great attention.[24] Though Scanderbeg only ruled over parts of northern and central Albania, he was a hero for all his people. To nineteenth century nationalists, Scanderbeg served as an example for their own century for uniting Albanians together in a common struggle against foreign domi-

---

[23]quoted in Kristo Frashëri, *Abdyl Frashëri* [In Albanian] (Tiranë, 1984), p. 144.

[24]For a comprehensive history of Scanderbeg in English, see A.K. Brackob, *Scanderbeg: George Castriota and the Albanian Resistance to Islamic Expansion in Fifteenth Century Europe* (Las Vegas: Vita Histria, 2018).

nation. Scanderbeg's struggle symbolizes the ethnic unity of the people which they wished to propagate; it also served their political goals by emphasizing Albanian resistance to the Ottomans as means of refuting the view prevalent in Europe that the Albanians were Turks.

The Albanians had long preserved the memory of Scanderbeg and his resistance to the Ottomans. For example, in 1636, Frang Bardhi, an Albanian bishop, published *George Castriota of Epirus, generally named Scanderbeg, very brave and invincible prince of the Albanians* to refute the claim of the Bosnian bishop that Scanderbeg was of Slavic and not Albanian origin.[25] Many of the nationalist leaders of the nineteenth century wrote works about Scanderbeg. The most important of these works include Zef Jubani's *History of Life and Deeds of George Castriota* (1878),[26] Jeronim de Rada's *The Unlucky Scanderbeg* (1884)[27] and Naim Frashëri's *The History of*

---

[25]Koli Xoxi, "Frang Bardhi (1606-1643)," in *Fjalor Enciklopedik Shqiptar,* p. 68.

[26]Jup Kastrati, "Zef Jubani (1818-1880)" in *Fjalor Enciklopedik Shqiptar*, p. 436; and *Historia e Shqipërisë*, II, p. 165.

[27]Jeronim De Rada, "Skanderbeg I pafan" in Jeronim De Rada, *Vepra Letrare*, 3 volumes, ed. Jup Kastrati (Tiranë, 1987), volume 2; and Koço Bihiku, *A History of Albanian Literature*, (Tirana, 1980), pp. 80-81.

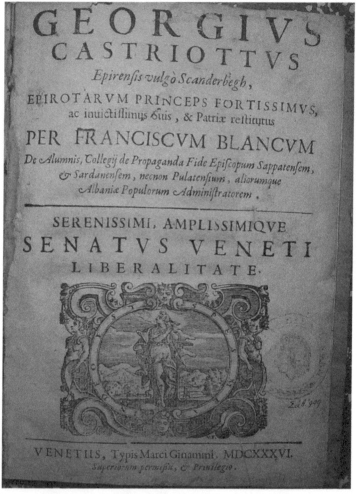

Title page of Frang Bardhi's George Castriota
of Epirus, generally named Scanderbeg,
very brave and invincible prince of the Albanians
published in 1636

Scanderbeg (1898).[28] Pashko Vasa used the example of Scanderbeg to emphasize the distinction between the Albanians and the Greeks. The fact that the Greeks did not assist Scanderbeg in his struggle against the Ottoman invaders, he argued, proved that the Albanians were a separate ethnic group from the Greeks.[29]

The legacy of the heroic struggle led by Scanderbeg, which has been preserved in the popular memory through legends and folk songs,[30] played a major role in the formation of the Albanian national consciousness. Edith Durham, the English anthropologist who traveled in Albania early in the twentieth century confirmed this when she remarked, "Skenderbeg is a great hero in his own land."[31]

History played an important political role during the years of the League of Prizren. When Abdyl Frashëri and Mehmet Ali Vrioni undertook their diplomatic

---

[28]Dhimitër Shuteriqi, "Naim Frashëri (1846-1900)" in *Fjalor Enciklopedik Shqiptar*, p. 289.

[29]Vasa, *Études sur l'Albanie*, p. 45.

[30]Dora d'Istria, "La nationalité albanaise d'après les chants populaires," pp. 382-418, in *Revue des Deux Mondes*, 68 (May-June, 1866), pp. 403-404.

[31]Mary Edith Durham, *The Burden of the Balkans* (London, 1905), p. 309.

mission on behalf of the League to Rome, Paris, London, Berlin and Vienna in the spring of 1879, seeking recognition of the national rights of the Albanians from the Great Powers of Europe, they brought with them pamphlets explaining the history, geography, and ethnography of the Albanian lands.[32] Frashëri relied upon history, asserting the antiquity of the people in their homeland and their strident resistance to the Ottomans, in attempting to influence European public opinion in support of the cause of the League of Prizren.[33]

Frashëri also used history to stress the non-aggressive aims of the national movement. In his famous "Letter from Janina," which was published in the journal *Basiret* in Istanbul on 12 April 1878, he wrote:

> The Albanians who in their nature are born with the virtues of heroism and bravery, have not been subordinate to any nation since the most ancient times because they themselves have never been conquerors.[34]

---

[32]Frashëri, *Abdyl Frashëri*, p. 241.

[33]Kristo Frashëri, "Skrimet politike të Abdyl Frashëri," pp. 65-103 in *Studime Historike*, 18:1 (1981), p. 98.

[34]quoted in Kristo Frashëri, *Tre Vëllezër Pishtare: Abdyl Frashëri, Naim Frashëri, Sami Frashëri* (Tiranë, 1978), p. 24.

Abdyl Frasheri
(1839-1892)

He sought to alleviate the fears of the European powers and the other Balkan states that an Albanian state would pursue a policy of territorial aggrandizement.

Frashëri emphasized the history of Albanian resistance to the Ottomans both during Scanderbeg's time and afterward. Late in his life, he wrote,

> The Albanian people are the only nation which has developed from time an energetic resistance against the Turkish occupation. This heroic resistance has continued until our day.... As a consequence, Albania merits independence more than any other nation of the Balkans and we hope that it will show itself worthy to enjoy the respect of Europe and most capable of governing itself.[35]

History was not only an important factor in the formation of the national consciousness, but also in asserting the national rights of the Albanians to the rest of Europe.

---

[35]quoted in Frashëri, *Tre Vëllezër Pishtare,* p. 36.

IV

Customs and Folklore
as a Source of National Identity

As was true of other Balkan peoples, an important aspect in the formation of an Albanian national consciousness was the study of customs and folklore. Folklore is a deep-rooted expression of the ethnic identity of any people and in it nineteenth century nationalists found an important connection with their people's past. The village was the principal repository of folklore. Due to the general isolation of the peasants from the wider world, they preserved this cultural heritage.

During the nineteenth century, the world was becoming a smaller place. As we have seen, the ambitions of the neighboring states and the centralizing reforms of the Ottoman Empire threatened the traditional way of life among the Albanians. For this reason, Albanian nationalists, like their Balkan counterparts, gathered folklore and recorded it to preserve the popular culture of their people and assure that it would not be lost.

Already in the seventeenth century, Frang Bardhi (1606-1643) made the first known attempt to gather Albanian folklore, when, as an appendix to his Latin-Albanian dictionary (1635), the Albanian bishop published a collection of proverbs.[36] Nineteenth century nationalists built upon this modest beginning. Influenced by romantic writers such as Goethe and Victor Hugo, the Albanians of Italy, known as the Arberesh, took an active interest in studying folklore. The most prominent intellectuals among the Arberesh were Jeronim de Rada (1814-1903) and Demetri Camarada (1821-1882), both of whom did extensive research into the folklore of their people.[37]

Another prominent intellectual who studied folklore, was a Romanian princess of Albanian descent, Elena Ghika (1829-1888). Writing under the pseudonym Dora d'Istria, she became the central figure of the

---

[36]Koli Xoxi, "Frang Bardhi (1606-1643)," in *Fjalor Enciklopedik Shqiptar*, p. 68.

[37]Bihiku, p. 77; Jup Kastrati, "Dhimitër Kamarada (Demetrio Camarada, 1821-1882)" in *Fjalor Enciklopedik Shqiptar*, p. 445; and Jeronim De Rada, *Vepra Letrare*, vols. 1 and 3.

Albanian national movement.[38] Her most important work, "La nationalité albanaise d'après les chants populaires," appeared in the French journal *Revue des Deux Mondes* in 1866.[39] Drawing upon the works of De Rada, Camarada, the Austrian scholar Johann Georg von Hahn, and others, she studied the Albanian nationality through popular folk songs.

Dora d'Istria asserted that these folk songs were an important repository of Albanian traditions and that they kept alive the memories of the popular heroes who fought the Turks, such as Scanderbeg. She wrote, "The double love of independence and of war, which is proclaimed in each line of these songs, gives the explanation of the whole history of these people since their defeat by Turkey and their enslavement by the Asiatic race."[40] As one of the most recognizable and respected figures of the national renaissance, Dora d'Istria's work was important in promoting the cause of Albanian nationalism throughout Europe. She was also

---

[38]Klara Kodra, "Dora d'Istria – historian luftëtare për lirinë e kombeve," pp. 79-86 in *Studime Historike*, 25:4 (1988), p. 80; and Vehbi Bala and Ahmet Kondo, "Elena Gjika (Dora d'Istria, 1829-1888)" in *Fjalor Enciklopedik Shqiptar*, pp. 341-342.

[39]Dora d'Istria, "La Nationalité Albanaise," pp. 382-418.

[40]Dora d'Istria, "La Nationalité Albanaise," pp. 391.

Elena Ghika (Dora D'Istria)
(1829-1888)

highly regarded by the Albanians themselves. In 1879, the French scholar Louis Benloew wrote that Dora d'Istria, "is surrounded by the veneration and enthusiastic affection of all the Albanians,"[41]

The Albanian Bee, published in Alexandria in 1878, is the best known collection of Albanian folklore from this period. It is a compilation of folk songs, tales, and proverbs from southern Albania gathered by Thimi Mitko (1820-1890). Mitko was born in Korça and emigrated to Egypt in 1859 where he became the most prominent nationalist figure among the Albanian colony in Cairo.

Mitko was a devout nationalist; in 1867, he wrote a poem which called for armed struggle to achieve national liberation.[42] He actively supported the struggle for autonomy, writing numerous articles to support the cause of his countrymen and adapting the "Marseillaise" to be the anthem of the League of Prizren.[43] Mitko's

---

[41]Louis Benloew, *Analyse de la langue albanaise: étude de grammaire compare*, (Paris, 1879), p. xi.

[42]Qemal Haxhihasani, "Thismi Koste Mitko (1820-1890)" in *Fjalor Enciklopedik Shqiptar*, pp. 713-714; and Qemal Haxhihasani, "Bleta shqiptare" in *Fjalor Enciklopedik Shqiptar*, pp. 104-105.

[43]Pollo and Puto, p. 130.

study of folklore furthered the development of the Albanian national consciousness. As Stavro Skendi observed, *The Albanian Bee*, "testified that the Albanian loved his countrymen, even if they belonged to other religions."[44]

Although both history and folklore were vital elements in the formation of the Albanian national consciousness, language was certainly the foremost aspect of this development. Nationalists generally regarded language as the most important expression of their national culture.[45] This was especially true among the Albanians who were divided by religion and territory.[46] The Albanian language, derived from ancient Illyrian, not only attested to the autochthony of the people in their land, but it was also the most visible factor

---

[44]Stavro Skendi, *The Albanian National Awakening, 1878-1912* (Princeton, 1967), pp. 121-122.

[45]Barbara Jelavich, *History of the Balkans: Eighteenth and Nineteenth Centuries* (Cambridge, 1983), p. 173.

[46]Kristo Frashëri, "Les pays des Albanais au XVe siècle," pp. 127-142 in *Deuxième Conference des Études Albanologiques* (Tirana, 1969), p. 133; Alfredo Uçi, "La ligue albanaise de Prizren et son facteur culturel dans la résistance nationale," pp. 117-136 in *Studia Albanica*, 15:1 (1978), p. 127; and Logoreci, p. 42.

uniting them and distinguishing them from their neighbors.

In the early 1900s, Edith Durham commented that, "In Albania it [Illyrian] never died out, but survives today as modern Albanian. And with the language has survived the fierce racial instinct, which to this day makes the Albanian regard the Slav as his first and worst foe."[47] The Albanians preserved their native tongue despite centuries of Ottoman rule and the spread of Islam among the people. Traveling in Albania in 1809-1810, John Cam Hobhouse observed that, "The Turkish language is known but to very few, even of the Mahometans amongst them."[48]

The first mention of the Albanian language comes from the travel account of French monk, Brochard, who wrote in 1332 that, "Although the Albanians have a language quite different from Latin, they use the Latin alphabet in all their books."[49] The famous chronicler Marin Barleti confirms the existence of written Albanian texts in his account of the siege of Shkodra when he

---

[47]Mary Edith Durham, *High Albania* (London, 1909), p. 4.

[48]Hobhouse, p. 144.

[49]quoted in Bihiku, p. 11. Bihiku argues that the author of this travel account is really the French Dominican Guillaume Adae, Archbishop of Antivari.

speaks of native chronicles recounting legends about the founding of the city.[50] Unfortunately, none of these early text survived. The earliest known Albanian text is a baptismal formula, using the Latin alphabet, written in 1462 by the Archbishop Paul Angelus.[51] The first known Albanian book did not appear until 1555 when Gjon Buzuku's *The Mass Book* was published. It was a translation of parts of the gospel and prayers of the Roman Catholic Church intended to aid local priests.[52] Albanian writings increased during the seventeenth century. Among the most important figures in the development of written Albanian during this period were Pjetër Budi (1566-1622), a bishop active in the struggle against the Ottoman occupation,[53] Frang Bardhi, who compiled a Latin-Albanian dictionary of 5,000

---

[50]Bihiku, pp. 11-12.

[51]Bihiku, p. 11.

[52]Stavro Skendi, "The History of the Albanian Alphabet: A Case of Complex Cultural and Political Development," pp. 211-232 in *Balkan Cultural Studies* (Boulder, 1980), p. 212; and Bihiku, p. 13.

[53]Shaban Demiraj, "Pjetër Budi (1566-1622)" in *Fjalor Enciklopedik Shqiptar*, p. 124; and Bihiku, pp. 13-14.

words (1635),[54] and Pjetër Bogdani (1625-1689), a cleric who adapted the Latin alphabet to Albanian and promoted the publication of books in his native tongue.[55] Despite the efforts of these men, a formal written language did not develop, thus William Martin Leake could rightfully claim at the beginning of the nineteenth century that, "The Shkipetaric, or Albanian, is not a written language."[56]

One of the difficulties in attempting to create a written language was that Albanian was not the language of instruction in the schools. The schools in Albania were all under foreign control. In the mid-nineteenth century, Albanian was only taught in two Roman Catholic schools in Shkodra, and in these only as a secondary subject, Italian being the language of instruction.[57] Moslem and Orthodox schools taught in Turkish and Greek.

One of the most influential educational institutions in Albania during this period was the Orthodox school

---

[54]Bihiku, p. 14; and Koli Xoxi, "Frang Bardhi (1606-1643)" *Fjalor Enciklopedik Shqiptar*, p.68.

[55]Bihiku, p. 15; and Durham, *High Albania*, p. 10.

[56]Leake, p. 260.

[57]Pollo and Puto, p. 115; and Skendi, *Albanian National Awakening*, p. 130.

Zosimea in Janina. This school was established in 1828 as a seven-year school, and in 1852 it became a gymnasium. It provided students with training in classical literature, theology, philosophy, history, and in addition to Latin and Greek, taught Persian, French, Italian and Arabic. This school produced some of the most important leaders of the Albanian national movement, including Jani Vreto, Konstandin Kristoforidhi, Ismail Kemal, and Naim and Sami Frashëri.[58] It was not until 1889, five years after the League of Prizren had been suppressed, that Naim Frashëri persuaded the Porte to allow the opening of the first Albanian school, in Korça.[59]

Circumstances were more favorable for the Albanians of Italy. The Arberesh had schools of their own and, already in 1794, an institution of higher education – Collegio di San Adriano in Calabria.[60] In 1848, Jeronim De Rada, the most prominent Arberesh intellectual, published the first Albanian newspaper,

---

[58]Dhimitër Beduli, "Zosimea," in *Fjalor Enciklopedik Shqiptar*, p. 1205.

[59]Stuart E. Mann, *Albanian Literature: An Outline of Prose, Poetry and Drama* (London, 1955), p. 37.

[60]Skendi, *Albanian National Awakening*, p. 116; and Stavro Skendi, "Millet System and its Contribution to the Blurring of Orthodox National Identity in Albania," pp. 187-204 in *Balkan Cultural Studies*, p. 196.

L'Albanese d'Italia, in Naples.[61] The Albanians of Italy provided important support for the formation of a national consciousness among their fellow countrymen across the Adriatic. They actively encouraged the national awakening in their homeland and lent material and financial assistance to the Albanian cause whenever possible.[62]

The nineteenth century witnessed a renewal of interest in the Albanian language. The first systematic analysis of the Albanian language was undertaken by foreigners. Albania, particularly southern Albania, attracted the attention of most of Europe during the Napoleonic Wars when Ali Pasha of Tepelena engaged in numerous diplomatic intrigues with the great powers of Europe in an attempt to gain independence for his province. This led the English scholar William Martin Leake to undertake the first serious study of the Albanian language in 1808.

Leake was not only interested in the antiquity of the language. "At the time these researches were made," he explained, "its dialect had received an additional claim to notice from the changes which had brought the country where it is spoken into contact with our own

---

[61]Bihiku, p. 30.

[62]Pollo and Puto, p. 114.

enemies, who then made no secret of their design of seeking a road through Albania into Greece. Under these circumstances it became doubly interesting to obtain some knowledge of the language."[63]

In his book, *Researches in Greece*, Leake outlined Albanian history and geography, provided a grammar with a Greek, English and Albanian vocabulary, using the Latin alphabet. This study was a difficult undertaking. He wrote:

> Though I had met with several Albanians of talent, and adequate learning, yet I never found one who had bestowed any attention of the grammar of his vernacular speech, or who had thought of any arrangements of rules, arising from that similarity of inflexion in the several parts of speech, which occurs in every language.[64]

Leake finally found a teacher, Evstratio of Viskuki, an Albanian who was an official in the Greek Orthodox Church and school master at Moshkopoli. Evstratio, who knew both Greek and Latin, taught Leake Albanian and assisted him with his study.[65] Though there is no evidence that Leake's work directly impacted the

---

[63]Leake, p. iii.

[64]Leake, p. 263.

[65]Leake, p. 263.

national movement, undoubtedly the interest in the Albanian language and culture that he and other foreigners, such as F. Pouqueville who commissioned Marko Boçari to write a Greek-Albanian dictionary in 1809,[66] demonstrated, exposed the Albanian intellectuals they met to ideas of nationalism and the importance of language as a defining element in ethnic identity. This type of influence is attested to later in the century when the Austrian consul in Janina, Johann Georg von Hahn, encouraged his language teacher, Konstandin Kristoforidhi, to undertake Albanian studies.[67]

The most important leader of the Albanian national movement in the early part of the nineteenth century was Naum Veqilharxhi. Veqilharxhi was born in Vithkuq, near Korça, in 1797. In 1806, while still a boy, he emigrated with his family to Romania, where he was exposed to ideas of nationalism and the enlightenment. Influenced by these ideas, Veqilharxhi joined the Greek revolutionary organization, *Filiki Hetaria*, and participated, along with many of his countrymen, in the rebellion of 1821 in the Romanian principalities led by

[66]Skendi, "The History of the Albanian Alphabet," p. 215.

[67]*Historia e Shqipërisë*, II, p. 169; Skendi, *Albanian National Awakening*, p. 122; and Xhevat Lloshi, "Konstandin Kristoforidhi (1827-1895)," in *Fjalor Enciklopedik Shqiptar*, p. 551.

Naum Veqilharxhi
(1767-1846)

Tudor Vladimirescu.[68] The exposure to ideas of nationalism and the practical political experience they gained in Vladimirescu's revolt, led Veqilharxhi and other Albanians living in Romania to begin to work for the cause of Albanian nationalism.

As a lawyer in Braila, Veqilharxhi became wealthy and used his money to promote the development of a national consciousness among his people.[69] He became part of an intellectual circle of Albanians in Braila who believed that the development of language and culture among their countrymen was a necessary prerequisite for Albania to become a modern nation.[70] As the Romanian historian Victor Papacostea observed, "Veqilharxhi and his companions formed a political group, the first of which in the century of nationalities was engaged in the struggle for the Albanian idea."[71]

---

[68]Victor Papacostea, "La participation de l'écrivain albanais Vechilhardji à la révolution de 1821," pp. 187-191 in *Balcania*, 8 (1945), pp. 190-191; and *Historia e Shqipërisë*, II, p. 134.

[69]Victor Papacostea, "Sur l'abécédaire albanais de Vechilhardji," pp. 248-252 in *Balcania*, 1 (1938), p. 249.

[70]*Historia e Shqipërisë*, II, p. 134; and Myslim Island, "Naum Veqilharxhi (Bredhi)" in *Fjalor Enciklopedik Shqiptar*, p. 1161.

[71]Papacostea, "La participation de l'écrivain albanais Vechilhardji," p. 191.

Western ideas of nationalism had a strong impact on Veqilharxhi. He expressed these clearly when he wrote, "The time has come to rouse ourselves and to reconsider our way of life, to change our course more radically and follow the example of the advanced nations throughout the world."[72] To do this, Veqilharxhi realized that the development of the written language was essential. Like other Albanian intellectuals, such as Pashko Vasa, he believed that education and the spread of culture were important prerequisites to any political struggle for national rights.[73]

As early as 1824, Veqilharxhi began compiling a special Albanian alphabet of 33 letters. He felt that rather than adopting the Latin, Arabic or Greek alphabets, the Albanian language should have a special alphabet of its own to testify to its unique character.[74] This alphabet also served a political purpose. It rejected the religious implications of the other three in an attempt to promote ethnic unity.

Using this alphabet, Naum Veqilharxhi published the first Albanian primer, *Evetor*, in Romania in 1844. The

---

[72]Quoted in Pollo and Puto, p. 109.

[73]Pollo and Puto, p. 111.

[74]*Historia e Shqipërisë*, II, p. 135; and Myslim Island, "Naum Veqilharxhi (Bredhi)," p. 1661.

The Alphabet Devised by Naum Veqilharxhi for the Albanian language alongside the modern equivalents

Vithkuqi	Modern	Vithkuqi	Modern	Vithkuqi	Modern	Vithkuqi	Modern	Vithkuqi	Modern	Vithkuqi	Modern
(glyph)	A a	(glyph)	V v	(glyph)	TH th	(glyph)	N n	(glyph)	T t	(glyph)	X x
(glyph)	:E ë	(glyph)	B b	(glyph)	Z z	(glyph)	NJ nj	(glyph)	F f	(glyph)	E e
(glyph)	I i	(glyph)	G g	(glyph)	K k	(glyph)	P p	(glyph)	H h	(glyph)	LL ll
(glyph)	O o	(glyph)	J i	(glyph)	Q q	(glyph)	R r	(glyph)	H h		
(glyph)	U u	(glyph)	DH dh	(glyph)	L l	(glyph)	S s	(glyph)	C c		
(glyph)	Y y	(glyph)	D d	(glyph)	M m	(glyph)	SH sh	(glyph)	Ç ç		

book was distributed in southern Albania in Veqilharxhi's home region of Korça and as far west as Berat
by Naum Hogi Basile. The book received an enthusiastic
welcome. In the spring of 1845, Veqilharxhi received a
letter from Athanase Pascali and others of Korça
requesting as many more copies of the book as possible
and proclaiming that, "Our nation will count, thanks to
this beginning, among the enlightened nations of
Europe."[75] This led Veqilharxhi to publish a second
edition of the work, *Fare i ri evetor shqip* [*Completely new
Albanian Primer*], in 1845. The enthusiastic response
which these first Albanian primers received is evidence
that a national consciousness had begun to form in the
Albanian lands.

Veqilharxhi was very encouraged. He travelled to
Istanbul in 1850 and tried to organize cultural society to
promote education and the printing of books in the
native language. The Porte and the Patriarch of the
Orthodox Church opposed his efforts to foster Albanian
culture. Both looked upon the Albanians as either Turks
or Greeks depending upon their religious affiliation and
they thwarted Veqilharxhi's efforts to create an Albanian

---

[75]quoted in Papacostea, "Sur l'abécédaire albanais," pp. 249-
250, which contains a complete version of the letter from the
Library of the Romanian Academy.

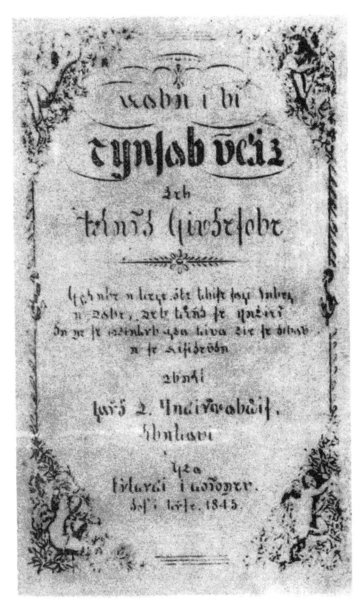

Cover of Veqilharxhi's primer, *Evetor*

cultural society. Finally, in 1854, he was poisoned by agents of the Patriarch.[76]

The murder of Veqilharxhi did nothing to impede the growth of the Albanian national consciousness. The work of Konstandin Kristoforidhi played a particularly important role in the development of a written language. Kristoforidhi was born in Elbassan, in central Albania, in 1827. While studying at Zosimea in Janina in 1847, he met the Austrian scholar Johann Georg von Hahn to whom he taught Albanian.[77] Hahn was an Austrian diplomat who took an active interest in studying Albanian language and culture; his most important work, *Albanesische Studien* (1853), is a study of the geography, history and ethnography of the country that also includes an Albanian grammar and a German-Albanian dictionary.[78] Hahn encouraged young Kristoforidhi to pursue Albanian studies – a task to which he devoted the rest of his life.

Kristoforidhi paid particular attention to the study of language. "If the Albanian language is not written," he argued, "in a short time there will be no Albania on

---

[76]Pollo and Puto, p. 111.

[77]*Historia e Shqipërisë*, II, p. 169; and Xhevat Lloshi, "Konstandin Kristoforidhi (1827-1895)," p. 551.

[78]Johann Georg von Hahn, *Albanesische Studien*, (Wein, 1853).

the face of the earth, nor will the name Albania appear on the map of the world."[79] In 1865, the Bible Society of London commissioned him to translate various parts of the Bible into Albanian. He used the Latin alphabet for his translations into the Geg dialect and the Greek alphabet for his translations into Tosk dialect[80] because the inhabitants of northern Albania were more familiar with the Latin alphabet due to the influence of the Roman Catholic Church, while residents of the south were more familiar with the Greek alphabet because of the influence of the Orthodox Church. In addition to his translations of the Bible, Kristoforidhi published several other works on the Albanian language, including primers in both the Geg and Tosk dialects,[81] but his life's work was the compilation of an Albanian dictionary.

Kristoforidhi intended his dictionary as a means to teach and spread the Albanian language. He traveled throughout the land, gathering words from all regions of

---

[79]quoted in *Historia e Shqipërisë*, p. 169.

[80]Skendi, "The History of the Albanian Alphabet," p. 214; Skendi, *Albanian National Awakening*, p. 122; Xhevat Lloshi, "Konstandin Kristoforidhi (1827-1895)," in *Fjalor Enciklopedik Shqiptar*, p. 551.

[81]Xhevat Lloshi, "Konstandin Kristoforidhi (1827-1895)" in *Fjalor Enciklopedik Shqiptar*, p. 551; and Émile Legrand, *Bibliographie Albanaise* (Paris, 1912), p. 113.

Albania. His work became legendary. Early in the twentieth century, Edith Durham heard the story of Kristoforidhi and recounted it in her book *The Burden of the Balkans:*

> A native of Elbassan, a patriot and enthusiast, he devoted some forty years of his life to the building of a monumental dictionary, collecting not only the main dialects, but visiting village after village in search of local words. He died in 1892, and bequeath to his son the manuscript, which is reported to have contained no less than forty thousand words. The Greek Consul at Durazzo offered young Kristoforidhi several thousand francs for the manuscript, and represented that his government wished to publish it. The Greek offer was accepted; the Consul received the manuscript. Far from paying for it, he denounced the young man to the Turks for national propaganda, and he was imprisoned for two years. The fate of the dictionary is unknown. A rumor was spread that the Greeks had destroyed it. Some believe it exists and will yet see the light of day.[82]

Kristoforidhi's dictionary was indeed published in Athens in 1904. It contained 11,675 words in Albanian

---

[82]Durham, *Burden of the Balkans*, p. 196.

and Greek, with notations indicating where the words were gathered or the author who used them.[83] The importance of Kristoforidhi's dictionary lies not in its contents, but in his method of compiling it. Traveling from village to village, inquiring into local language usage, he helped to make people aware of the importance of language as part of their ethnic identity, thereby enhancing the development of the Albanian national consciousness. That the legend of Kristoforidhi and his dictionary was widespread in Albania at the turn of the century attests to this fact.

The establishment of a uniform alphabet was a fundamental problem that had to be overcome to develop a written language. Some intellectuals, like Zef Jubani and Hasan Tahsini, argued, as had Naum Veqilharxhi earlier, that since the Albanian language was linguistically unique, it should have its own special alphabet.[84] Other nationalists, such as Jani Vreto, argued that the Greek alphabet should be adopted to stress the ties between the Albanian and Greek peoples as the earliest inhabitants of the Balkan peninsula.[85] Moslem

---

[83]Xhevat Lloshi, "Fjalor i gjuhës shqipe i K. Kristoforidhit" in *Fjalor Enciklopedik Shqiptar*, p. 275.

[84]*Historia e Shqipërisë*, II, p. 165.

[85]Skendi, *Albanian National Awakening*, p .139.

leaders, supported by the Ottoman government when the ban on printing in Albanian was lifted in 1878, favored the Turko-Arabic script as a means of protecting Islamic culture and Ottoman influence in Albania.[86] The Latin alphabet was favored by the Arberesh and the Catholics of northern Albania. Nationalists such as Ismail Kemal and Pashko Vasa advocated the Latin alphabet for the very practical reason that the letters were more readily available for printing.[87] The issue would not be settled until November 1908, when the Congress of Manastir established the modern Albanian alphabet using Latin characters.

Albanian intellectuals recognized the overwhelming need to establish a uniform alphabet and grammar for their language.[88] Sami Frashëri expressed this sentiment to Jeronim De Rada when he wrote, "The Albanian language should be one and indivisible, just as Albania

---

[86]Ligor K. Mile, *Kryengritjet Popullore në fillim të Rilindjes sonë, 1830-1877* (Tiranë, 1962), p .211.

[87]Skendi, *Albanian National Awakening*, p. 139; *Historia e Shqipërisë*, II, p. 172.

[88]"Thimi Mitko to Jeronim De Rada, 13 January 1879, Dok. II/5," in "Documents sur la ligue albanaise de Prizren," pp. 167-225 in *Studia Albanica*, 15:1 (1978), p. 199; and "Jeronim De Rada to Elana Gjika, 1870," in Jeronim De Rada, *Vepra Letrare*, vell. 3, pp. 325-326.

should be."[89] In 1864, Konstandin Kristoforidhi, Pashko Vasa, Ismail Kemal, and Hasan Tahsini attempted to create a cultural society in Istanbul to encourage the opening of Albanian schools and the publication of books in their native tongue. Their efforts, like those of Veqilharxhi, were hampered by interference from the Porte and the Patriarch, and plagued by disputes over what alphabet should be adopted.[90] In 1871, these Albanian intellectuals, along with Jani Vreto and Sami Frashëri, attempted to form a new cultural association and to pressure the Porte to allow the opening of Albanian schools. Again their efforts were rebuffed because of opposition from the Porte and the Patriarch.[91] The proclamation of the Ottoman constitution by Sultan Abdulhamit II on 12 December 1876 revived the hopes of Albanian nationalists of opening schools in their country. Kristoforidhi requested that the Porte recognize the Albanian language and allow the opening of schools, but Grand Vezir Midhat Pasha refused to accede to his demands.[92] Only during the crisis of 1878, when the Ottoman government hoped for Albanian support in its

---

[89]Quoted in Skendi, *Albanian National Awakening*, p. 120.

[90]*Historia e Shqipërisë*, II, p. 169

[91]*Historia e Shqipërisë*, II, p. 172; and Pollo and Puto, p. 115.

[92]Pollo and Puto, p. 115.

Sami Frasheri (1850-1904)
together with his wife Emine

attempts to preserve the territorial integrity of the Empire, did the Porte yield to the most basic demand of the Albanian nationalists and officially recognize their language.

The leaders of the League of Prizren realized the need to continue efforts to develop a written language to enhance popular support for their program of territorial and administrative autonomy.[93] The first step in this direction was the creation of an alphabet. The League created a committee to establish an alphabet for the printing of Albanian books in Istanbul in March, 1879; among the members of this committee were such prominent intellectuals as Sami Frashëri, Jani Vreto, Pashko Vasa and Hasan Tahsini.[94] The committee adapted the Latin alphabet to Albanian by including some additional letters. This became known as the Alphabet of Istanbul. Despite the efforts of the League's

---

[93]Uçi, p. 118; and "Dok. 107, Zëri i Shqipërisë, Athinë, nr. 4, 20 tetor 1879," in *Mendimi Politike Shoqëror i Rilindjes Kombëtare Shqiptare, Vëllimi I, 1879-1908*, ed. Zihni Haskal (Tiranë, 1971), pp. 227-228, which argues for education in the Albanian language.

[94]Uçi, p. 119; and Ahmet Kondo, "Alfabetarja e gjuhës shqipe – veper e rendesishme për përhapjen e ideve kombëtare," in *Konference Kombëtare e Studimeve për Lidhjen Shqiptare te Prizrenit, II, 12-28 qershor 1978*, (Tiranë, 1981), p. 198.

cultural program, this alphabet did not become universal. What is significant is that the League chose the Latin alphabet as the basis for written Albanian and in doing so laid the groundwork for the modern alphabet which is also based on Latin characters.

Pashko Vasa was one of the most prominent advocates for the adoption of the Latin alphabet for written Albanian. His pamphlet, *L'alphabet latin applqué à langue albanaise,* was published in Istanbul in 1878.[95] In addition to the practical reason that Latin letters were readily available for printing, Vasa argued that the adoption of the Latin alphabet would assert that Albania was part of the broader European cultural community.[96] Use of the Latin alphabet was also an important way of distinguishing the Albanians from their Ottoman rulers, as well from their Slavic and Greek neighbors. The Latin alphabet also served a political purpose by providing a common bond between the Albanians and the Great Powers of Europe, such as Britain and France, from

---

[95]Pashko Vasa, *L'alphabet latin appliqué à la langue albanaise,* (Constantinople, 1878).

[96]Tomor Osmani, "Alfabeti i Pashko Vases," pp. 87-94 in *Alfabeti i Gjuhës Shqipe dhe Kongresi i Manastirit, 14-22 nëntor 1908: studime, material, dokumente* (Tiranë, 1972), p. 88; and Mile, p. 211.

Pashko Vasa
(1825-1892)

whom the nationalists hoped to gain support in their struggle for autonomy.

This was certainly Pashko Vasa's goal when he later devised a new alphabet, again based on Latin, and used it in a grammar published in England in 1887.[97] This alphabet was an important precursor of the modern Albanian alphabet as only 8 of its 35 characters were different: zh for c; c for ç; é for e; e for ë; l for ll; rh for rr; x for zh; and zh for x.[98] The creation of the Alphabet of Istanbul and the work of Pashko Vasa resolved that the Latin alphabet would eventually be officially applied to Albanian, but its specific form would not be determined for thirty years. The adoption of the Latin alphabet furthered the development of the national consciousness because it distinctly marked that the Albanian language, and thereby the Albanian people, were a unique nation, unrelated to their Slavic and Greek neighbors. The efforts by Albanian intellectuals to stress this fact were an important part of their attempts to protect the territorial

---

[97]W.P. [Pashko Vasa], *Grammaire Albanaise à l'usage de ceux qui désirent apprendre cette langue sans l'aide d'un maître* (London, 1887).

[98]Osmani, p. 92. See p. 94 for a chart comparing the two alphabets.

integrity of their lands and assert the national rights of their people.

Having temporarily resolved the issue of the alphabet, on 12 November 1879, the leaders of the League of Prizren founded the Society for the Printing of Albanian Letters, with Sami Frashëri as its president. Other prominent members included Pashko Vasa, Jani Vreto, Hasan Tahsini, and Zija Prishtina.[99] The purpose of this organization, which served as the cultural wing of the League, was to print books for Albanian schools to further the development of the national consciousness. This sentiment was expressed in the preamble to the constitution of the Society:

> All enlightened nations have been… civilized by writing in their own language. Every nation that does not write in its own language and has no works in it is in darkness and barbarian. And the Albanians, not writing their own language and having no works in their own language, are in the same state…. Therefore, those who think and see this great calamity are also aware of the great need to write their language and read works in it.[100]

---

[99]*Historia e Shqipërisë*, II, pp. 267-268.

[100]quoted in Skendi, *Albanian National Awakening*, p. 120.

Using its new alphabet, the society published a primer which it intended to disseminate to the schools it hoped to open. The society also published two journals, *Drita* [*The Light*] and *Dituria* [*The Knowledge*] to promote the Albanian cause.[101] Despite the suppression of the League of Prizren by the Ottomans, its cultural activities persisted. In 1881, Jani Vreto established a branch of the Society in Bucharest. After the Ottoman government reimposed the ban on Albanian books in 1885, Bucharest became the center of the Society's activities.[102]

Though on the surface the successes achieved by Albanian intellectuals in trying to develop a uniform alphabet and grammar for their language may appear small, they were significant and necessary steps in the formation of the Albanian national consciousness. By fostering the development of the language, a common bond was forged among the people that overcame regional and religious differences. This achievement must not be underestimated. Traveling in Albania

---

[101]Cristo A. Dako, *Albania, the Master Key to the Near East* (Boston, 1919), p. 82; Uçi, p. 119; and Skendi, "The History of the Albanian Alphabet," p. 216.

[102]Mann, pp. 35-36; and Kristo Frashëri, *The History of Albania* (Tirana, 1964), p. 146.

shortly after the turn of the century, Edith Durham observed:

> the knowledge of reading and writing the language is spreading rapidly. You find it in very unexpected quarters, and as a common bond of sympathy it is knitting together all classes of the people. Papers printed in London, in Rome, in Sofia, and Bukarest are smuggled in and read by Moslems and Christians alike all over the land. A literary language shows signs of developing.[103]

As an element binding the people together as a distinct nation, the development of a written language became the most important manifestation of the Albanian national consciousness.

---

[103]Durham, *The Burden of the Balkans,* p. 196.

V

The Problem of Religious Division

I f language was one of the key elements uniting the people, religion was one of the most significant factors dividing them. Nearly 70% of Albanians were Moslems, while 20% were Greek Orthodox and 10% Roman Catholic.[104] The need to overcome the problem of religious division distinguished Albania from the other Balkan nations where national churches played an important role in the formation of a national consciousness, helping to unite the people together as a nation. Albanian intellectuals tried to distance themselves from the religious establishments in the country and stressed the cultural unity of the people regardless of which faith they professed.

The problem of religious division was not as difficult to overcome as it might appear at first glance. Over the centuries, religion had only a minor influence

---

[104]Nicolae Iorga, *Brève histoire de l'Albanie et du people albanais* (Bucarest, 1919), pp. 67-68.

in Albanian life owing to the rural character and geographic isolation of the country. Both Christianity and Islam were imposed upon pre-existing pagan beliefs. The English anthropologist Edith Durham observed:

> The cross or the verses of the Koran are simply amulets. Under all lies a bedrock of prehistoric paganism, which has, perhaps, more influence in their lives that either of the other two.[105]

Albanian nationalists stressed that cultural unity bound together people of different faiths. Pashko Vasa wrote of the limited influence of religion in fundamentally altering the basic customs of the people:

> Independently of so many other religious practices which are related to the ancient cult of Pelasges and which neither Christ nor Mahomet have made completely disappear from the minds of the Albanian people, there is the oath on the stone which exists and is still used in all the mountains of Albania.[106]

The limited influence of religion in the country regularly impressed foreign visitors. Commenting upon

---

[105]Durham, *The Burden of the Balkans*, p. 207.

[106]Vasa, *Études sur l'Albanie*, p. 31.

the numerous conversions to Islam, William Martin Leake wrote:

> such of the Albanians, as have renounced Christianity, have done it entirely from political motives, and for the sake of enjoying Turkish dignities, and other advantages derived from professing the governing religion... their laxity of religious practice is a common subject of ridicule among the Turks.[107]

T.S. Hughes made a similar observation when he wrote in 1830 that:

> the Albanian Mahometan is not more observant of doctrines, rites, and ceremonies under his new law than he was under his old one, and is looked upon with great contempt by the rigid Osmanli.[108]

This casual attitude toward organized religion greatly assisted the development of the Albanian national consciousness, despite the religious division of the country. "Among the Albanians themselves," Edith Durham wrote, "there is no religious hatred."[109] Because the people did not define themselves by faith, the

---

[107]Leake, pp. 250-251.

[108]T.S. Hughes, *Travels in Greece and Albania*, volume 2, (London, 1830), p. 105.

[109]Durham, *The Burden of the Balkans*, p. 257.

religious division of the country was not an insurmountable obstacle for the development of a national consciousness. Edith Durham related:

> In face of a common foe, Moslem and Christian Albania unite. Some nations have a genius for religion. The Albanians, as a race, are singularly devoid of it. Their Mohammedism and their Christianity sit but lightly upon them, and in his heart the wild mountaineer is swayed more by unwritten beliefs that date from the world's well-springs.[110]

Despite the limited effects of religious division in most parts of Albania, nationalist leaders still had to take the problem seriously. In the cities and among ruling class Moslem officials, religion was a more important factor than among the peasants. Albanian intellectuals realized that overcoming religious division would further strengthen the growing sense of national consciousness.[111] The principal way they did this was to stress Albanian culture and offer patriotism as a substitute for religious belief. Pashko Vasa's poem, *Mori*

---

[110]Durham, *The Burden of the Balkans*, p. 204.

[111]Mile, p. 216; and Myslim Islami, "Naum Veqilharxhi (Bredhi)," p. 1161. Veqilharxhi wrote a circular calling upon the Albanians to overcome religious division.

Shqypni a mjera Shqypni [*O Albania, poor Albania*], is one example of this:

> *Awake, Albanians, from age-long slumber*
> *On church and mosque rely no longer,*
> *You owe no duty to priest and pope,*
> *To love your country is your only hope.*

His proclamation that, "*The religion of the Albanians is Albanianism,*"[112] became the motto of the League of Prizren. Other attempts to stifle the effects of religious division included Sami Frashëri's call for the establishment of an Albanian Orthodox Church to free it from Greek and Slavic domination,[113] and Naim Frashëri's support for the Bektashi, a pantheistic Moslem sect which incorporated many elements of Christianity, as a means of achieving a religious unification.[114] Though these nineteenth century nationalists failed to eliminate the religious divisions, their attempts to do so strengthened the development of national consciousness

---

[112]quoted in Bihiku, p. 60; Pashko Vasa, *Vepra Letrare* (Tiranë, 1987), vëll. 1, pp. 37-39; and Mile p. 216.

[113]Skendi, "The Millet System," p. 199.

[114]Mann, pp. 38-40; Bihiku, p. 40; F.W. Hasluck, *Christianity and Islam under the Sultans*, ed. Margaret Hasluck (Oxford, 1929), vol. 2, p. 436. On Bektashiism, see John Kingsley Birge, *The Bektashi Order of Dervishes*, (London, 1965), pp. 215-216.

Naim Frasheri
(1846-1900)

as people became aware of the factors separating them and realized the need to overcome these obstacles to preserve their ethnic identity.

In addition to the problem of religious division, the fact that Albanians were predominantly Moslems led many Europeans to equate them with the Ottomans. Kirby Green, the British Consul-General for northern Albania, expressed this attitude when he described the League of Prizren to Edward Knight in 1879:

> Priserin, let me tell you, is the headquarters of the Albanian League, an organization of the most fanatical Mussulmen of the country, whose object is to resist the Austrian advance, and the Montenegrin claims by force of arms. These men are now worked up to high pitch of religious zeal, and hatred of the Christians. Preserin is, with perhaps the exception of Mecca, the most dangerous spot for a Christian in all Mohammedan countries.[115]

This outlook was due in part to a general ignorance about the culture and history of the Albanian people, as well as the propaganda efforts of neighboring Balkan states intent on strengthening their territorial claims by denying the existence of the Albanian nation. After

---

[115]Knight, p. 115.

traveling through the country and meeting members of the League, Knight encountered a different view; "We are fighting for our independence," they told him, "There are as many Christians in the League as Mussulmen."[116] To gain support for their cause in Europe, Albanian leaders had to demonstrate that religion was not a fundamental aspect of their national character.

To make the rest of Europe recognize the Albanian nationality and to get them to stop viewing Albanians in religious terms, the leaders of the League of Prizren sought to educate Europe about the history and culture of Albania. The newspaper *I foni tis Alvanis* [*The Voice of Albania*], which was published in Athens in 1879-1880, emphasized that the Albanians were one nation, instead of three separate religious groups.[117] Pashko Vasa, in his work *Études sur l'Albanie et les Albanais*, proclaimed to the people of Europe:

> To call the Albanians Moslems and Catholics who do not belong to the Greek Church and to claim that thee Orthodox of the same country are Greeks

---

[116]Knight, p. 203.

[117]Zihni Reso, "L'activité d'A. Kullurioti dans son journal 'La Voix de l'Albanie' Durant les années dela Ligue de Prizren," pp. 43-66 in *Studia Albanica*, 15:2 (1978), p. 59.

because they profess the doctrine of the Orthodox Church, is in our opinion, to want to erect religious belief on the principal of nationality and to substitute dogma for race, religion for fatherland, which is not admissible.[118]

The most important political effort to promote the rights of the Albanian nation during this period was the League's diplomatic mission to the Great Powers of Europe, led by Abdyl Frashëri and Mehmet Ali Vrioni during the spring of 1879. They traveled to European capitals, insisting that language, not religion, defined the Albanian people. Applying this principle, Frashëri and Vrioni argued against the Greek annexation of the mainly Orthodox region of Arta in southern Albania because the ethnic composition of the region was Albanian.[119] With foreign governments controlling the fate of their land, the efforts of Albanian intellectuals to obtain international recognition of the national rights of

---

[118]Vasa, *Études sur l'Albanie,* p. 61.

[119]"Dok. 18, Telegram i Safet pashës dërguar Karatheodhor pashës për bisedën e Abdyl Frashërit dhe Mehmet Vrionit me ministrin e Punëve të Jashtme të Francës, Vaddington, 9 maj 1879," pp. 36-38 in *Lidhja Shqiptare e Prizrenit në Dokumentet Osmane, 1878-1881,* ed. Kristaq Prifti (Tiranë, 1978).

their people was a critical element in their struggle to achieve autonomy and to preserve the territorial integrity of their land.

VI

The Formation of a
National Consciousness

H aving examined the role of history, folklore, language and religion in the formation of the Albanian national consciousness, the question as to how nationalist ideas were disseminated throughout this rural and mountainous land must be considered. By the time of the creation of the League of Prizren in 1878, these ideas had spread among the peasants who enthusiastically rallied behind the cause of preserving the territorial integrity of their lands.[120] As we have already seen, the efforts of intellectuals like Konstandin Kristoforidhi, who traveled from village to village collecting words for his

---

[120]Stefanaq Pollo, "La lutte du people albanais sous la 'Ligue de Prizrend' pour la libération nationale," pp. 29-48 in *Studia Albanica*, 5:2 (1968), p. 36.

dictionary, were one important way that ideas of nationalism spread among the rural population.

Economic development was another important factor in the formation of a national consciousness among the rural population. The Tanzimat reforms encouraged the penetration of foreign capital into Albania, helping to begin a process of integration into the European economy.[121] Nevertheless, the Albanian economy remained essentially quasi-feudal. Capitalist relations of production, as such, had little influence before the twentieth century; thus, the formation of a national consciousness did not coincide with the growth of a bourgeois class.[122]

Despite this, Albania experienced significant economic growth during the nineteenth century. This is evidenced by the growth of cities and an increase in the size of the local markets. In the period from 1830-1840 to 1900-1912, the size of cities grew by an average of 37%, while the number of shops in the bazaars increased by 56%.[123] The peasants from the surrounding countryside

---

[121]Zija Shkodra "Aspects du marché albanaise Durant la période de la renaissance nationale," pp. 93-128 in *Studia Albanica*, 15:2 (1978), p. 96.

[122]Mile, p. 50

[123]Shkodra, p. 112.

came to the local bazaar to trade livestock, grain, and handicrafts. These centers not only brought the peasants into contact with one another, but also with the wider world. The bazaar was not only an economic center, but also a social and political center where the peasants encountered ideas of nationalism. Edward Knight observed that, "this crowded mart is the common rendezvous, and answers for the purpose of a club."[124] The assassination of Mehmet Ali, an Ottoman official sent to Albania in 1878 to convince the League to comply with the decisions of the Congress of Berlin and to relinquish Plava and Gucia to Montenegro, illustrates the significances of the bazaar as a political center. Knight recorded:

> His death was decided on by the League. The projected murder was talked about freely in the bazaars of Albania fully two weeks before it was perpetrated."[125]

The growth of the internal market brought the peasants into closer contact with one another and the bazaars served as important centers for the diffusion of nationalist ideas among the rural population.

---

[124]Knight, p. 135.

[125]Knight, p. 219.

Political struggle is another decisive factor in creating conditions favorable for the coalescence of a national consciousness. Social and political struggles enhanced the development of a national consciousness by creating conditions which favored its growth. The intellectual aspects of the formation of a national consciousness could not be complete without a corresponding political element. A nation is, after all, a social, cultural and political unit.

Many Albanian intellectuals gained extensive political experience by participating in the national movements of other European peoples; for example, his participation in the Romanian rebellion of 1821 influenced Naum Veqilharxhi,[126] and many Arberesh intellectuals, including Jeronim De Rada, took part in the Italian liberation movement.[127] Pashko Vasa's book, *Burgimi Im* [*My Imprisonment*], tells of his participation in the Venetian uprising against Austrian rule in 1848. In it, he reveals that the democratic and nationalist ideas of the revolt had a strong influence upon him. "The future is of the people," he wrote, "and the people of Venice are

---

[126]Mile, p.213.

[127]Jup Kastrati, "Mbi rolin e Arbëreshëve të Italise në periudhen e Lidhjes Shqiptare," pp 196-203 in *Konferenca kombëtare e studimeve për Lidhjen Shqiptare të Prizrenit, 1878-1881, I, 12-28 qershor 1978* (Tiranë, 1979), p. 200.

great, worthy to be imitated and honored by the whole world."[128]

The intellectual aspects of the formation of a national consciousness gave added strength to the social and political struggles. Peasant resistance to Ottoman rule had recurred at different times throughout the centuries, but the formation of a national consciousness enhanced its effectiveness by creating a common bond among people from different regions.

Already in 1847, the impact of the developing national consciousness upon the popular resistance movement could be seen. That year, several local rebellions broke out in southern Albania in opposition to military recruitment and a new tax on cattle. These rebellions spread rapidly and peasant armies besieged Ottoman garrisons at Berat and Gjirokastra. What set this rebellion apart from previous ones was that communications were established between the leaders of these local uprisings and they established a central coordinating committee to guide the activities of the

---

[128]Pashko Vasa, "Burgimi Im," pp. 137-293 in Pashko Vasa, *Vepra Letrare* (Tiranë, 1987), p. 284.

rebels.[129] The developing sense of national consciousness served as a foundation for the political struggle.

Despite the defeat of this rebellion, it contributed to furthering the development of national conscious-ness because it showed people the benefit of uniting together against their common foes and helped to spread nationalist ideas among the participants of the uprising. This experience proved valuable when the struggle to preserve the territorial integrity of the Albanian lands began in earnest in 1878.

The formation of the Albanian national consciousness during the decades prior to the crisis of 1878 created the basis for a national movement. The League of Prizren was a political, military and cultural association. Writing in the journal *Courrier de l'Orient* in 1878, Sami Frashëri proclaimed that the League was an organization of patriots, inspired by political and not religious ideals.[130] The League not only sought to prevent the annexation of Albanian lands by neighboring states, but also to compel the Ottoman government to unite the

---

[129]Pollo and Puto, pp. 110-111; Mile, p. 150; and *Historia e Shqipërisë*, II, p. 133.

[130]Zija Xholi, "Sami Frashëri – patriote, démocrate et scientifique éminent," pp. 19-42 in *Studia Albanica,* 21:1 (1984), p. 23.

four Albanian vilayets into a single province with an autonomous administration. They demanded that the Albanian language be used in the administration of the province and the schools.[131] Albanian leaders viewed autonomy as a step toward national independence and an essential part of their program to protect the territorial integrity of their lands.

While the Ottomans initially supported the League as a means of influencing the decisions made at the Congress of Berlin, this situation soon changed as the Albanians refused to comply with the decisions of the Porte and to confine their interests to preserving the territorial integrity of the Empire. This was apparent as early as August 1878, when the League refused requests from the Porte to send troops to Bosnia to oppose the Austrian advance there.[132] Then, the League ordered the

---

[131]Selami Pulaha, "Le programme de la Ligue albanaise de Prizren pour la formation de la province automne de l'Albanie," pp. 27-42 in *Studia Albanica,* 15:2 (1978), p. 40; Stavro Skendi, "Beginnings of the Albanian Nationalist and Autonomous Trends: The Albanian League, 1878-1881," pp. 219-232 in *The American Slavic and East European Review,* 12:2 (April, 1953), p. 226; and L.S Stavrianos, *The Balkans since 1453* (New York, 1958), p. 503.

[132]Pollo and Puto, p. 120; and Skendi, *Albanian National Awakening,* p. 56.

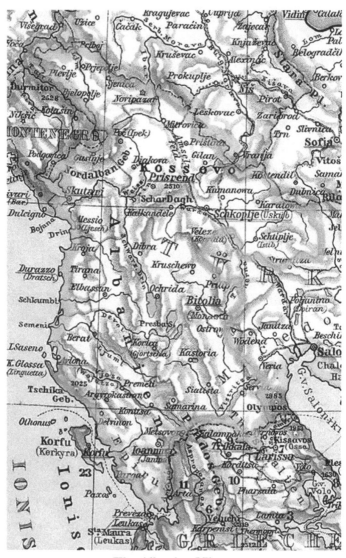

The Albanian Vilayet
proposed by the League of Prizren

assassination of the Sultan's representative, Mehmet Ali, on 6 September 1878.[133] A year later, Edward Knight observed:

> Defense of their native land against foreign invasion is now not their only cry; but autonomy, the shaking off of the Turkish yoke are boldly discussed in the bazaars of the garrison towns.[134]

Prior to their break with the Porte, Albanian leaders, such as Pashko Vasa, stressed that they wanted to maintain their union with the Ottoman Empire, and that they only sought autonomy within it.[135] They believed that autonomy under the Empire would give them time to prepare for national independence. The disputes between the League and the Porte over implementation of the decisions of the Congress of Berlin led many to begin thinking of establishing an independent state. "I tell you we will have the Turks no more. The chiefs of the League have sworn it," one League member told Edward Knight. "Independence has been given to Montenegro – to Bulgaria. Albania shall have her independence, and

---

[133]Pollo and Puto, p. 120; and Skendi, *Albanian National Awakening*, p. 57.

[134]Knight, p. 259.

[135]Vasa, *Études sur l'Albanie*, pp. 97-97 and 107.

the great powers shall recognize us."[136] The League of Prizren became full-fledged movement for national independence. Despite its failure to achieve its goals during this time, it laid the groundwork for the establishment of an independent Albanian nation-state in 1912.

---

[136]Knight, p. 202.

Conclusion

The formation of the Albanian national consciousness during the period preceding the formation of the League of Prizren was critical to the creation of this national movement. The national consciousness did not suddenly develop in response to the crisis of 1878. As we have seen, this process began in the early part of the nineteenth century. Intellectual leaders such as Naum Veqilharxhi, Konstandin Kristoforidhi, and Pashko Vasa played a critical role in the creation of a national movement to prevent the partitioning of Albanian lands among the neighboring Balkan states. Their efforts fostered the development of the Albanian national consciousness.

Despite the repression of the League of Prizren by Ottoman forces in the spring of 1881, the national struggle of the Albanian people to preserve their territory and culture enhanced their sense of national consciousness. The temporary reestablishment of Ottoman political control could not blunt this achievement. Thus, the formation of the Albanian national consciousness in the period preceding the crisis of 1878 was of vital importance for the future of the people by creating the basis for the foundation of the Albanian nation-state in 1912.

Bibliography

Alfabeti i Gjuhës Shqipe dhe Kongresi i Manastirit, 14-22 nëntor 1908: studime, material, dokumente. Tiranë, 1972.

Benloew, Louis. *Analyse de la langue albanaise: étude de grammaire compare.* Paris, 1879.

Bihiku, Koco. *A History of Albanian Literature.* Tirana, 1980.

Birge, John Kingsley. *The Bektashi Order of Dervishes.* London, 1965.

Brackob, A.K. *Scanderbeg: George Castriota and the Albanian Resistance to Islamic Expansion in Fifteenth Century Europe.* Las Vegas, Oxford, Palm Beach, 2018.

Chekrezi, Constantine A. *Albania: Past and Present.* New York, 1919.

Dako, Cristo A. *Albania, the Master Key to the Near East.* Boston, 1919.

d'Istria, Dora. "La nationalité albanaise d'après les chants populaires," pp. 382-418 in *Revue des Deux Mondes* (May-June, 1866).

"Documents sur la ligue albanaise de Prizren," pp. 167-225 in *Studia Albanica*, 15:1 (1978).

Durham, Mary Edith. *The Burden of the Balkans*. London, 1905.

Durham, Mary Edith. *High Albania*. London, 1909.

Fjalor Enciklopedik Shqiptar. Tiranë, 1985.

Frashëri, Kristo. *Abdyl Frashëri* [In Albanian]. Tiranë, 1984.

Frashëri, Kristo. "Les pays des Albanais au XVe siècle," pp. 127-142 in *Deuxième Conference des Études Albanologiques*. Tirana, 1969.

Frashëri, Kristo. "Skrimet politike të Abdyl Frashëri," pp. 65-103 in *Studime Historike*, 18:1 (1981).

Frashëri, Kristo. *The History of Albania*. Tirana, 1964.

Frashëri, Kristo. *Tre Vëllezër Pishtare: Abdyl Frashëri, Naim Frashëri, Sami Frashëri*. Tiranë, 1978.

Gilbert, Frederic. *Les pays d'Albanie et leur histoire*. Paris, 1914.

Hahn, Johann Georg von. *Albanesische Studien*. Wein, 1853.

Haskal, Zihni, ed. *Mendimi Politike Shoqëror i Rilindjes Kombëtare Shqiptare, Vëllimi I, 1879-1908.* Tiranë, 1971.

Hasluck, F.W. *Christianity and Islam under the Sultans.* Ed. Margaret Hasluck. Oxford, 1929.

Hasluck, Margaret. *The Unwritten Law in Albania,* ed. J.H. Hutton. Cambridge, 1954.

Hobhouse, John Cam. *A Journey through Albania and other Provinces of Turkey in Europe and Asia, to Constantinople, during the years 1809 and 1810.* London, 1813.

Holland, Henry. *Travels in the Ionian Isles, Albania, Thessaly, Macedonia, & a. during the years 1812 and 1813,* Volume 2. London, 1819.

Hughes, T.S. *Travels in Greece and Albania.* 2 volumes. London, 1830.

Iorga, Nicolae. *Brève histoire de l'Albanie et du people albanais.* Bucarest, 1919.

Jelavich, Barbara. *History of the Balkans: Eighteenth and Nineteenth Centuries.* Cambridge, 1983.

Kastrati, Jup, ed. *Jeronim De Rada, Vepra Letrare.* 3 volumes. Tiranë, 1987.

Kemal, Ismail. *The Memoirs of Ismail Kemal Bey.* Ed. Sommerville Story. London, 1920.

Knight, Edward. *Albania: A Narrative of Recent Travel.* London, 1880.

Kodra, Klara. "Dora d'Istria – historian luftëtare për lirinë e kombeve," pp. 79-86 in *Studime Historike*, 25:4 (1988).

Konferenca kombëtare e studimeve për Lidhjen Shqiptare të Prizrenit, 1878-1881, I, 12-28 qershor 1978. Tiranë, 1979.

Konferenca kombëtare e studimeve për Lidhjen Shqiptare te Prizrenit, II, 12-28 qershor 1978. Tiranë, 1981.

Leake, William Martin. *Researches in Greece.* London, 1814.

Legrand, Émile. *Bibliographie Albanaise.* Paris, 1912.

Logoreci, Anton. *The Albanians; Europe's Forgotten Survivors.* London, 1977.

Magno, Stefano. "Événements historique en Grèce (1479-1497)," pp. 214-243 in *Documents inédit relatifs à l'histoire de la Grèce au Moyen Age*, Tome VI, ed. C.N. Sathas. Paris, 1884.

Mann, Stuart E. *Albanian Literature: An Outline of Prose, Poetry and Drama.* London, 1955.

Mile, Ligor K. *Kryengritjet Popullore në fillim të Rilindjes sonë, 1830-1877.* Tiranë, 1962.

Papacostea, Victor. "La participation de l'écrivain albanais Vechilhardji à la révolution de 1821," pp. 187-191 in *Balcania*, 8 (1945).

Papacostea, Victor. "Sur l'abécédaire albanais de Vechilhardji," pp. 248-252 in *Balcania*, 1 (1938).

Pipeneles, Panagiotes. *Europe and the Albanian Question*. Chicago, 1963.

Pius II. "The Commentaries of Pius II: Book VI-IX," trans. Florence Alden Gragg, *Smith College Studies in History*, Volume 35. North Hampton, MA, 1951.

Pollo, Stefanaq, ed. *Historia e Shqipërisë*, vëlle. 2. Tiranë, 1984.

Pollo, Stefanaq. "La lutte du people albanais sous la 'Ligue de Prizrend' pour la liberation nationale," pp. 29-48 in *Studia Albanica*, 5:2 (1968).

Pollo, Stefanaq, and Arben Puto, *The History of Albania*, trans. Carol Wiseman and Ginnie Hole. London, 1981.

Pouqueville, F.C.H.L. *Travels through the Morea, Albania and several other parts of the Ottoman empire to Constantinople during the years 1798, 1799, 1800 and 1801*. London, 1806.

Prifti, Kristaq, ed. *Lidhja Shqiptare e Prizrenit në Dokumentet Osmane, 1878-1881*. Tiranë, 1978.

Pulaha, Selami. "Le programme de la Ligue albanaise de Prizren pour la formation de la province automne de l'Albanie," pp. 27-42 in *Studia Albanica,* 15:2 (1978).

Puto, Arben. "La ligue albanaise et la crise orientale," pp. 95-116 in *Studia Albanica,* 15:1 (1978).

Reso, Zihni. "L'activité d'A. Kullurioti dans son journal 'La Voix de l'Albanie' Durant les années dela Ligue de Prizren" pp. 43-66 in *Studia Albanica,* 15:2 (1978).

Shaw, Stanford. *History of the Ottoman Empire and Modern Turkey,* Volume 2. New York, 1976.

Shkodra, Zija. "Aspects du marché albanaise Durant la période de la renaissance nationale," pp. 93-128 in *Studia Albanica,* 15:2 (1978).

Skendi, Stavro. "Beginnings of the Albanian Nationalist and Autonomous Trends: The Albanian League, 1878-1881," pp. 219-232 in *The American Slavic and East European Review,* 12:2 (April, 1953).

Skendi, Stavro. *The Albanian National Awakening, 1878-1912.* Princeton, 1967.

Skendi, Stavro. "The History of the Albanian Alphabet: A Case of Complex Cultural and Political Development," pp. 211-232 in *Balkan Cultural Studies.* Boulder, 1980.

Skendi, Stavro. "Millet System and its Contribution to the Blurring of Orthodox National Identity in Albania," pp. 187-204 in *Balkan Cultural Studies*. Boulder, 1980.

Stavrianos, L.S. *The Balkans since 1453*. New York, 1958.

Uçi, Alfredo. "La ligue albanaise de Prizren et son facteur culturel dans la résistance nationale," pp. 117-136 in *Studia Albanica*, 15:1 (1978).

Xholi, Zija. "Sami Frashëri – patriote, démocrate et scientifique éminent," pp. 19-42 in *Studia Albanica*, 21:1 (1984).

Vasa, Pashko [Wassa Effendi]. *Études sur l'Albanie et les Albanais*. Constantinople, 1879.

Vasa, Pashko [W.P.], *Grammaire Albanaise à l'usage de ceux qui désirent apprendre cette langue sans l'aide d'un maître*. London, 1887.

Vasa, Pashko. *L'alphabet latin appliqué à la langue albanaise*. Constantinople, 1878.

Vasa, Pashko. *Vepra Letrare*. Tiranë, 1987.

Index

A

Abdulhamit II, Sultan, 63

Adae, Guillaume, 45

Adriatic Sea, 19, 49

Albanesische Studien, 58

Albanian alphabet, 54, 55,
61, 62, 65, 68

Albanian Bee, The, 43, 44

Albanian dictionary, 59, 60

Albanian independence,
1912, 92, 94

Albanian language, 22, 25,
32, 45, 47, 49, 50, 54, 58,
59, 61-63, 65, 68-70, 89

Albanian League. *See*
League of Prizren

Albanian origins, 32

Albanian Orthodox
Church, 77

Albanian Rebellion of
1481, 19

Albanianism, 77

Alexander the Great, 19

Alexandria, 43

Ali Pasha, 49

Ali, Mehmet, 85, 91

Alphabet of Istanbul, 65,
68

Angelus, Paul, 46

Antivari, 45

Arabic alphabet, 54, 62

Arabic language, 48

Arberesh, 40, 48, 62, 86

Arta region, 81

Athens, 60, 80

Austria, 31, 51, 58, 86, 89

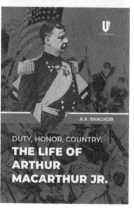
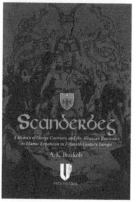